Getting To Know...

Nature's Children

MOOSE

Judy Ross

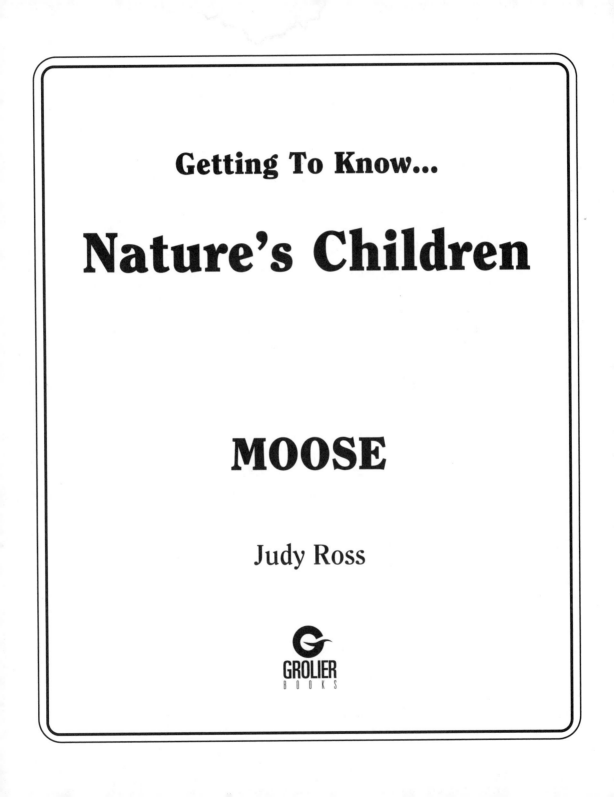

GROLIER
B O O K S

Facts in Brief

Classification of the Moose

    Class: *Mammalia* (mammals)

    Order: *Artiodactyla* (cloven-hoofed mammals)

    Family: *Cervidae* (deer family)

    Genus: *Alces*

    Species: *Alces alces*

World distribution. Found in northern regions of Europe, Asia, and North America.

Habitat. Northern forested lands near lakes or streams; may summer on the northern tundra.

Distinctive physical characteristics. Large palmate antlers on male; long legs; back slopes downward from high shoulders; bell-shaped fold of skin hangs under throat.

Habits. Solitary in summer; gathers in small bands in winter; swims in lakes to eat underwater plants; female raises calves (usually two) alone.

Diet. Leaves, twigs, bark, grasses, herbs, water plants.

Edited by: Elizabeth Grace Zuraw
Design/Photo Editor: Nancy Norton
Photo Rights: Ivy Images

ISBN: 0-7172-8778-5

Have you ever wondered . . .

What comes to your mind when you think of a moose? Some people think of a coat-rack because the moose's upturned *antlers*—the huge bony growths on its head—look like a good place to hang a coat. Other people think of stilts because the moose's body is perched on top of long skinny legs.

A coat-rack on stilts! But if that's the way *you* think of a moose, you're in for a big surprise.

Moose may look awkward and clumsy, but don't be fooled by appearances. These animals are so agile they can disappear gracefully into dense forests without even making a sound.

Let's find out more about this striking member of the deer family.

Few animals in North America are as impressive as the long-legged moose. And the male has antlers that sometimes have been known to measure as much as 6 feet (1.8 meters) across.

Awkward Beginning

For the first few days of its life, a baby moose, or *calf,* has trouble getting around on its skinny, stilt-like legs. They wobble and buckle under the little moose, causing it to stagger unsteadily. But the calf gets stronger and steadier on its feet every day. By the time it's a week old, the calf might be able to beat you in a foot race. It also can swim, even at that early age.

A calf must become strong and steady on its feet very quickly so that it can run if danger threatens. After all, it doesn't yet have strong legs to kick with, or antlers it can use to scare off its enemies.

At birth, a baby moose's long legs are shaky, but soon the calf is able to run faster than you can.

Moose Turf

Opposite page:
A moose has big shoulders that form a hump, making the hindquarters much lower than the shoulders.

Most moose live in the forested areas on the edge of the Arctic in North America and Eurasia. But the *habitat* of some moose is found farther south, often near lakes or streams. A habitat is the place where an animal lives. Some moose even live in the treeless northern tundra, where the winters are often very cold.

The shaded area on this map shows where moose live in North America.

All in the Family

Moose are the largest members of the deer family. They're at least a head taller than their cousins—the elk, deer, and caribou. The male, or *bull,* is larger than the female, or *cow.* He can weigh as much as 1,200 pounds (535 kilograms) and stand more than 6 feet (2 meters) tall.

How can you tell the difference between a bull and a cow moose when you can't compare their size? It's easy. Only male moose have antlers.

Even though a female moose is smaller than the male, she is still as large as a horse!

Heavy Headed

Imagine walking, running, and even swimming with a piano bench tied to your head. Sound impossible? Not for a bull moose. A fully grown bull moose's antlers can easily be about the size and weight of a piano bench! But while you might have trouble carrying around something so large and heavy, the moose doesn't even seem to notice its cumbersome headgear. It can lope easily through dense forest without smashing its antlers on trees or getting them stuck in branches.

Male moose don't start life with a handsome pair of antlers. During their first year, they grow only tiny brown buttons, the beginnings of antlers. The next year, the antlers are a bit bigger and they stick out like handles on either side of the moose's head. Finally, after seven years of bigger and bigger antlers, the male's headgear is fully grown.

Opposite page: Waiting seven years for a full pair of antlers may seem like a long time, but it's just as well. What a staggering load a baby moose would have to carry if it suddenly sprouted a pair of antlers the size of a piano bench!

Shreds of torn velvet still cling to the antlers of this moose. Some moose antlers can weigh as much as 80 pounds (36 kilograms).

Something's Missing

Male moose don't have antlers all year round. In early winter their antlers drop off. Often one antler is shed before the other, so the moose has to get used to being lopsided for a few days.

In early spring a new set of antlers sprouts. First tiny black knobs appear. These knobs are covered with a soft fuzzy skin called *velvet*. This velvet contains blood vessels to nourish the antlers and help them to grow.

By mid-July, the antlers are full size, and in early fall the velvet begins to fall off. During this stage the moose looks quite messy, with strips of ragged velvet hanging from its head-gear. To help loosen this fuzzy skin, the moose often rubs its antlers against trees.

Comparison of moose and elk antlers

Moose

Elk

The Big Stretch

Opposite page: *A moose's long legs come in handy. When threatened, the animal can kick out with either its front or hind hoofs—and it doesn't often miss its target!*

A moose is so tall that a three-year-old child would reach only to the animal's knobby knees. The moose's long thin legs account for most of its height. Having long legs is a big advantage for a forest dweller. They allow a moose to step easily over logs on the ground, reach up into trees for food, and wade through deep snow that would stop other animals.

If you're ever lucky enough to see a moose in the wild, stop and watch how it moves. It strides majestically through the trees and over fallen logs without slowing its pace. A moose on the move is a very graceful creature indeed.

The moose's long legs are also useful when it needs to defend itself or escape from an enemy. It can kick out to fend off a hungry wolf or, if that fails, it can outrun an attacker.

Like other members of the deer family, the moose has split *hoofs* for feet. A hoof is a hard covering of horn. As the moose walks over swampy ground, the split hoofs spread out slightly, providing more support for the moose's big, bulky body.

Sight, Sounds, and Scents

A moose's sleepy-looking, big brown eyes may be one of the animal's most handsome features, but a moose has very poor eyesight. Luckily its other senses are much sharper.

Its big ears are like those of a mule. Whenever a moose hears something that may mean danger, its ears stand up on end to catch the sound waves. Thanks to these effective sound catchers, a moose can hear much better than we can.

A moose uses its big nose to sniff the air. Its keen sense of smell can pick up the windblown scent of other animals long before the moose can actually see them.

With ears and a nose this big, hearing and smelling are two of the moose's strongest senses.

Moose tracks

Water Lover

Moose like to be near water where they can find food and escape from danger. They're strong swimmers and have even been known to dive underwater in search of a tasty plant. When a moose dives underwater, its *nostrils,* or nose openings, close to keep the water out of its nose, just as a submarine's hatches close before it submerges, to prevent water from pouring into the sub.

A river or lake is also a handy escape from black-flies and mosquitoes. In summer, a moose will stand neck deep in water to keep these pesky insects from biting it.

Water makes up an important part of the moose's habitat. Moose are often seen in or near it.

Big Eaters

It sometimes seems that a moose's day is just one long meal. In summer, juicy green leaves, twigs, and plants make up most of its diet, but its favorite food is water lilies. Much of a moose's water-lily munching takes place in the early morning or late in the afternoon. The moose stands partially submerged in the water and dips its nose under to tear the lilies from their stems.

This moose didn't have to wade in very deep to indulge in its favorite treat—water lilies.

During winter, when water plants are not available, the moose eats twigs. A full-grown moose may chow down 40 to 50 pounds (18 to 23 kilograms) of twigs a day. At the end of the winter, when a moose has already eaten most of the twigs it can reach, it may tear strips of bark off trees and eat that.

It's easy to tell if a moose has been feeding nearby. The trees will be twigless up to a height of several yards (meters). That's as high as a hungry moose can reach.

The word moose *is an Algonquin Indian word that means "twig eater."*

Cud Chewers

Like all of its deer family relatives, a moose is a *cud chewer.* This means that a moose chomps down food while it wanders around, but waits until it can rest quietly before chewing the food properly. A moose can do this because part of its stomach acts as a "storage tank" for unchewed food. When the animal rests, it brings the food, called *cud,* from this storage place into its mouth. Then it can chew in peace. On a hot summer day, a moose often lies down in a shady spot to chew its cud. In winter, it may just flop down in the snow.

A moose's menu includes leaves and tender twigs. With its long legs, this tall animal can easily reach high branches.

Winter Woolies

Many animals build nests, make *dens,* or dig *burrows* for homes. A den is an animal home made in a cave, near a fallen tree, or in some other cozy place. A burrow is a hole dug in the ground by an animal for use as a home. But when it comes to a home for a moose, this animal does none of these things. A moose wanders from place to place in search of food and sleeps wherever it happens to be. That may sound fine in summer, but what happens when winter comes?

Although the moose doesn't have a den to snuggle up in, it has no problem staying warm. It grows a thick two-layered fur coat in the late fall. An outside layer of *guard hairs* sheds ice and snow and keeps out cold winds. Beneath that, a layer of thick *underfur* keeps the moose's body heat from escaping into the cold air.

Even a moose baby has no problem staying cozy all winter. It's warmed by its thick fur coat—and its mother, always close by.

Moose Groups

Moose live alone most of the year, but sometimes in winter they gather in small groups to search for food. They scratch at the snow with their front hoofs to dig out bits of plants or roots. It doesn't take long before the snow gets tramped down by a group of moose. These flattened areas are called *yards.* But even in yards, the moose keep their distance—though they may feed near each other. And one rule always applies: The strongest and largest moose always get first choice of the best food.

Opposite page:
In the summer, water plants are a steady item on the moose menu.

Mating Season

For moose, fall is *mating season,* the time of year during which animals come together to produce young. Moose *courtship,* or behavior before mating, is a noisy and sometimes dangerous affair. To let a male know she's interested, a female bellows loudly. If two bulls hear her call, they may fight to win her. These fights often involve much clanging and smashing of antlers. But usually the weaker bull backs off before anyone gets hurts.

Overleaf:
It's a head-on collision when two bull-moose rivals meet.

A Moose Nursery

In the spring, the cow moose goes off by herself to find a place to give birth to her calves. She is very fussy about a nursery. It must be well hidden from *predators,* animals that hunt other animals for food. To insure safety, the mother moose looks for a spot among bushes and trees, usually at the water's edge where the trees are dense. An island makes a good, safe nursery. In this hidden spot, the cow gives birth to her calves. Usually she has twins, but sometimes she may have as many as three babies, or possibly only one.

A newborn moose calf weighs 22 to 35 pounds (10 to 16 kilograms)—about the weight of a large dog. The first sounds that the baby utters are low grunts, but soon it's calling loudly to its mother with a sound much like a human baby's cry.

A moose calf is born without spots, one of the few members of the deer family to do so.

From Wobble to Walk

For a few days, the moose calf lies on the soft ground in the secret hiding place, sleeping and *nursing,* or drinking milk from its mother's body. At first, the mother cuddles and nuzzles her calf with her soft, rubbery nose. But soon she begins to nudge it to get up and walk.

During the first year of life, moose calves and their mother are seldom apart.

First Outing

When it's about three days old, the moose calf is ready to venture out for a walk with its mother. It wobbles unsteadily behind her as she browses for food near thick bushes. If danger approaches, she will nudge her baby into the bushes, safely out of sight.

Before long the calf will begin nibbling on tender shoots and young buds on bushes and trees. And by fall, it'll no longer need to drink its mother's milk.

A moose calf's fur is reddish-brown. Adult moose are brownish-black, with lighter fur on their legs and belly.

Young Swimmer

If you ever see two moose swimming, look closely. One is probably a baby moose. A moose calf can swim when it's only a few days old, but it's not yet a strong swimmer. From time to time it may rest its chin on its mother's back until it has enough strength to paddle on its own again.

Moose are completely at home in the water. One day these twins will be powerful swimmers.

Watchful Mother

Wolves and bears see little moose calves as tasty dinners—so a mother moose must be especially careful to protect her babies. She relies on her keen senses of smell and hearing to alert her to any approaching danger.

If her calf is threatened, the cow moose lowers her head and snorts loudly like a horse. Then she may rear up on her hind legs and paw the air. If this display doesn't frighten off the enemy, she'll kick out with her long, strong legs and sharp front hoofs. Those legs are powerful weapons. A moose can cripple a wolf with one well-placed kick. And even if the calf's own father comes near, he'll get the same treatment as other intruders. A mother moose trusts no one near her babies.

A young calf will stay with its mother for at least one year before venturing off on its own.

Survival Lessons

Moose in the wild may live to be 20 years old, but there are many dangers and hardships they have to face along the way.

During its time with its mother, a calf learns all of the lessons it'll need to survive. It watches how its mother pulls up tender water lilies, and then it does the same thing. It also watches its mother so that it can learn which trees have good twigs and bark to eat. And whenever danger threatens, it learns how to fight off enemies. It even learns how to escape pesky flies and mosquitoes by hiding in the water. All of these lessons are important for a young calf. Only by learning them well will it be able to survive.

A moose's long legs and short neck make it difficult for the animal to reach its mouth all the way down to the ground. In order to get a drink, a moose usually just wades into the water.

Leaving Home

The moose calf grows quickly, and by its second spring it's ready to go off on its own. When it leaves, its mother begins to search for a hiding place to give birth to her next set of babies.

A female calf can be a mother herself at age three. A male calf won't mate until he's five or six years of age. That's when his antlers will be big enough for him to challenge other males in a mating contest. Until then, a young moose lives alone, wandering through the forest as it chomps twigs in the winter. And in the summer, too, it wanders, stopping now and then for a cooling dip in a lake and a water-lily snack.

Words To Know

Antlers   Hard, bony growths on the head of male moose.

Bull   Male moose.

Burrow   A hole dug in the ground by an animal for use as a home.

Calf   A baby moose.

Cow   Female moose.

Cud   Hastily swallowed food brought back up for chewing by cud chewers such as deer, cows, and moose.

Den   An animal home.

Guard hairs   Long coarse hairs that make up the outer layer of a moose's coat.

Habitat   The area or type of area in which an animal or plant naturally lives.

Hoof, hoofs   The hard covering of horn on the feet of moose, cattle, deer, and some other animals. Sometimes the plural of hoofs is spelled hooves.

Mating season   The time of year during which animals come together to produce young.

Nostrils   The openings in the nose that let air in.

Nurse   To drink milk from a mother's body.

Predator   Animals that hunt other animals for food.

Tundra   Flat land in the Arctic where no trees grow.

Underfur   Short, dense hair that traps body-warmed air next to an animal's skin.

Velvet   Soft skin that nourishes and covers a moose's antlers while they grow.

Yard   An area where moose gather in winter to find food.

Index

PHOTO CREDITS
Cover: J. D. Markou, *Valan Photos.* **Interiors:** William Lowry, 4, 17. /*Valan Photos:* Murry O'Neil, 7; Brian Milne, 13; Joseph R. Pearce, 21; Dennis W. Schmidt, 29, 38; J. D. Markou, 30; Thomas Kitchin, 32-33; Stephen J. Krasemann, 36-37, 42; Wayne Lankinen, 45. /*Ivy Images:* Norman R. Lightfoot, 9; Don Johnston, 22-23. /Bill Ivy, 10, 18, 26, 40-41. /*Visuals Unlimited:* Ron Spomer, 14; Rod Kieft, 25. /*Canada In Stock / Ivy Images:* Mario Madau, 34.

Getting To Know...

Nature's Children

DOWNY
WOODPECKER

Katherine Grier

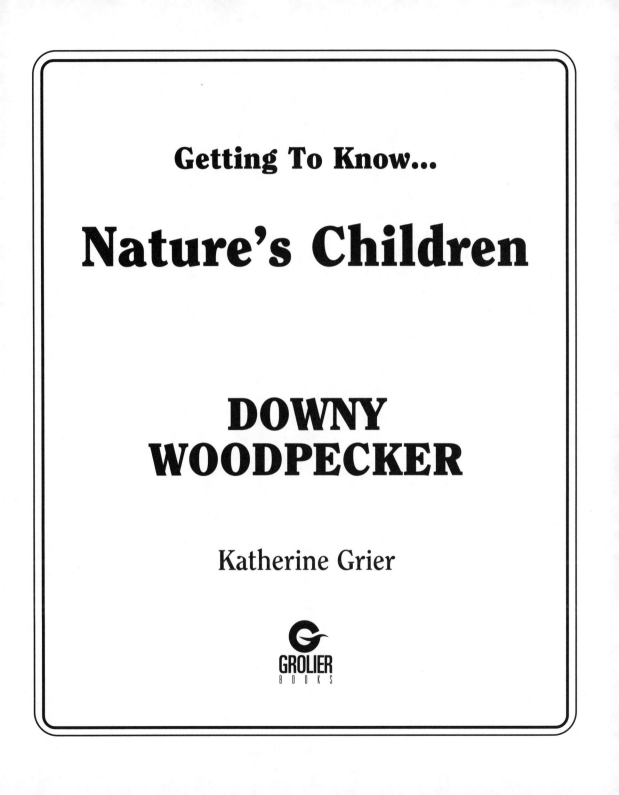

GROLIER
B O O K S

Facts in Brief

Classification of the Downy Woodpecker

    Class: *Aves* (birds)
    Order: *Piciformes* (woodpeckers)
    Family: *Picidae*
    Genus: *Dendrocopos*
    Species: *Dendrocopos pubescens*

World distribution. Exclusive to North America.

Habitat. City suburbs, orchards, and woods.

Distinctive physical characteristics. Sharp pointed bill; white back and belly; black wings with white stripes; red spot on the head of the male.

Habits. Mates for life; taps as a means of communication as well as to find food; nests in holes in dead trees; generally lays four or five eggs at a time.

Diet. Insects and some vegetation.

Edited by: Elizabeth Grace Zuraw
Design/Photo Editor: Nancy Norton
Photo Rights: Ivy Images

ISBN: 0-7172-8779-3

Have you ever wondered . . .

Have you ever wondered . . .

Downy Woodpeckers

Have you ever heard a busy drumming sound coming from a nearby tree or pole? Did you follow it, trying to figure out exactly where the sound was coming from? If you did, you might have found a small, red-headed bird rapping on the wood with its bill. Yes, to us that rapping sound usually means, "Look, and you may just spot a woodpecker!"

Perhaps you've wondered what a woodpecker is doing when it raps or pecks. And doesn't all that knocking with its bill hurt its head? Maybe you've even thought that woodpeckers aren't quite like other birds—and on that point you'd be quite right.

Woodpeckers are specially suited to life in the trees. We'll find out just how by looking at one kind of woodpecker that you're likely to see in your neighborhood, whether you live in the country, town, or city. It's a small, lively woodpecker that's not afraid of people. It's the Downy Woodpecker.

Opposite page:
A fairly short bill and a pattern of black and white feathers make a Downy easy to spot—but only the male has a red patch on its head.

A Long Way Down

A young Downy Woodpecker pokes its head out of the hole in the tree where it was born. It's hungry, but it can't fly yet, so it's looking for its mother and father who usually feed it. Behind the little Downy in the nest, its brothers and sisters call out hungrily, too. Where is dinner?

The young Downy sees its parents perched on a distant branch. Why aren't they coming with a new supply of food? Then suddenly a fly buzzes past. The hungry young Downy can't resist it. It reaches out to grab this tasty bug snack in its bill and…ooops! The Downy is out of the nest and fluttering down to the ground. It's the young bird's first flight!

The Downy Woodpecker parents look on from their perch. They know their young won't leave the nest unless they have a good reason. And what better reason is there than food? They watch for their next hungry baby to try its wings.

Downy Relatives

The Downy Woodpecker belongs to a big family. There are 179 different *species,* or kinds, of woodpeckers living around the world. Twenty-two species live in North America, and the Downy is one of them.

All woodpeckers have several things in common. They're all good climbers. They all use their bills to poke or dig for their food. And they all can use their bills to make holes for their nests.

Just as people look different, so do the Downy's relatives. Some are as big as crows, while others are as tiny as sparrows. Some are black and white, while others have bright green feathers. And there are woodpeckers of many other colors, too.

The different kinds of woodpeckers like different things to eat. Many eat insects they find on the ground or in trees. Some lap up the sap that flows from holes they make in tree trunks. And others prefer acorns, storing a supply for the winter in holes they dig in the bark of trees.

Getting to Know the Downy

The Downy Woodpecker is a small wood-pecker. It weighs only about 1 ounce (28 grams) when fully grown. This is about as much as an eraser weighs. The Downy measures about 6 inches (15 centimeters) from its head to the tip of its tail.

The Downy is a handsome bird. It has a bright white chest, a white stripe down its back, and black wings that have white checks and stripes. The male has a small red patch on the back of its head. The female has a patch in the same spot, but hers is black or white.

Copycat Cousin

The Downy's distinctive *markings,* or patterns and color of feathers, should make this bird easy to recognize. But there's one problem. One of its cousins, the Hairy Woodpecker, has almost the same markings. If you were to put a Downy and a Hairy Woodpecker side by side, you'd see that the Hairy Woodpecker is much bigger. But since you usually see a woodpecker by itself, this size test doesn't always work.

The best way to tell if a woodpecker is a Downy is to look at its bill. The Hairy Woodpecker's bill is about as long as its head, while the Downy Woodpecker's bill is much shorter—about half that length.

Compare this Hairy Woodpecker's long bill with that of a Downy. Unlike most woodpeckers, the Downy has quite a short and stubby bill.

At Home on Its Range

Opposite page:
Downy Wood-
peckers depend
on trees to
provide food as
well as places to
carve out a home.

Downy Woodpeckers live all over North
America—that is, wherever there are trees.
They make their home in city parks and
backyards, and in farm orchards and open
woodlands.

Every Downy lives on its own *range,* a
large area of land that provides the Downy its
food and shelter. In it there are sure to be
deciduous trees, trees that lose their leaves in
the fall. There the Downy can find insects and
larvae to eat. Larvae are the worm-like forms
of insects, also called *grubs.* The range also
provides dead or dying trees in which the
Downy can chisel out a place to sleep or a
nest hole for its young.

In spring and summer, the Downy shares a
range with a mate and raises a family. In fall
and winter it lives alone on its own range. The
Downy lives on the same range year after
year. It gets to know where favorite trees or
stumps are, how to get from one spot to
another, and where the best eating and
hiding places are.

A Friendly Neighbor?

In fall and winter when the Downy lives by itself, it doesn't get upset if other birds come into its range. In fact, being a small wood-pecker among many larger birds, the Downy sometimes doesn't have much choice.

Downy and Hairy Woodpeckers—which look so much alike—sometimes even share the same trees. The larger Hairy Woodpecker searches the main trunk for food, using its longer, stronger bill to chisel holes in hard live wood. The smaller Downy finds soft dead limbs to dig in. It moves easily among the smaller branches, looking for insects near the bark's surface. Because the two woodpeckers look for food in different places, they live side by side in peace. A Downy will also share its range with another Downy.

But when a Downy couple start making their nest and getting ready to raise a family, watch out. They're anything but friendly neighbors. They want to be left alone. In fact, they'll drive other birds, even other Downy Woodpeckers, out of their range.

Opposite page: *A Downy's favorite place to live is open wood-land. This bird is not commonly found in dense or thickly forested areas.*

A Downy Diet

The Downy gets much of its food by eating insects that crawl on the bark of trees. Many insects can move fast, but so can the Downy. It hops quickly through its favorite feeding places—small trees and the upper branches and twigs of big trees—snatching bugs where it finds them. Its favorites are beetles, beetle larvae, ants, caterpillars, and other small insects.

The Downy eats some fruits and berries, too—when it can find them. Raspberries, black-berries, cherries, and even the berries of poison ivy and poison sumac are common foods on this bird's menu. The Downy will also drink sap from the holes that its relative, the Sapsucker Woodpecker, taps deep into live trees.

The Downy's eating habits change with the seasons. In spring and summer when there are lots of insects, a Downy can eat well just by looking for them on top of the bark. But in fall and winter, it must get insects that live under the tree bark. That's when the Downy has to tap for its meal.

Tap-tap-tapping for Food

How does the Downy get at insects that have
tunneled into tree wood or telephone poles?
First it chisels into the wood to open up the
tunnels. It does this by hammering its straight
sharp bill into the wood over and over again.
Although the Downy's bill is made mostly of
hard bone, it's not as long or strong as many
other woodpeckers' bills. For that reason, the
Downy usually digs into softer dead or dying
wood for an insect dinner.

Getting the insects out of their tunnel homes
is no problem either. The Downy uses its
tongue to "fish" them out. A Downy's tongue
is long enough to probe deep into the tunnels.
And the tongue has yet another useful feature:
On its tip are tiny barbs that work like a fish-
hook. When the Downy reaches an insect, the
barbs hold it fast. The tongue is sticky, too,
which helps hold the insect. Then the Downy
draws its tongue back into its bill with the
bug attached.

Opposite page:
*Clamped firmly to
the bark of a tree,
this Downy is
ready to dig into
dinner. The job is
made easy by the
Downy's sharp
bill and a spear-
like tongue that
can shoot out two
inches or even
more to scoop up
tasty treats.*

A Protected Body

Opposite page:
The Downy leans on its tail for extra support when it drums on a tree.

Would you rather catch a baseball with your bare hand or a padded glove? Probably a padded glove. The Downy uses padding, too. It drums its bill against a tree more than 100 times a minute, but its head doesn't get hurt because it's protected. A Downy's bill is wide at the base. In addition, the bones of its skull are thick and heavy, and the muscles around its head and neck are strong. Together, the bill, skull, and muscles spread and absorb the force of the blows to protect the Downy's head from injury.

When the Downy chisels into a tree trunk, the air is filled with fine powder and flying chips of wood. You'd think that its *nostrils,* or nose openings, would get clogged, and that it would have a hard time breathing. But the Downy's nostrils, which are at the base of its bill, are covered with fine feathers. These feathers work as a filter and keep out all the wood dust, enabling the Downy to breathe in only clear air.

A Downy bill

Treetop Eating

Holding onto a tree and eating at the same time might not sound like your idea of a picnic, but it's a snap for a Downy.

Like most woodpeckers, the Downy is well-equipped for climbing straight up trees. It has four long toes on each foot, two pointing forward and two backward. Each toe ends in a sharp, curved nail that gives the Downy a good grip.

The Downy's tail also helps it, both when it's climbing and when it stops to eat. The feathers in its tail are pointed and stiff. The Downy leans back against them, using them as a prop.

Two pairs of toes— one pointing forward and the other to the back—give the Downy a very firm grip.

Hook-like feet enable a Downy to cling expertly to the rough bark of trees.

Keeping Clean

Opposite page:
*A Downy's molt
is so gradual that
it almost passes
unnoticed.*

The Downy works hard, but it also takes time to relax. *Preening,* or keeping its feathers well tended, is one way the Downy takes it easy. Each Downy has a special high stump or tree branch that is its favorite preening place.

There the Downy uses its bill to poke deep down among its feathers, cleaning away dirt and tiny *parasites,* insects that live on an animal. The Downy straightens some feathers by pulling them carefully through its bill. In between preening, the woodpecker tends to its feathers by shrugging its shoulders and fluffing and lifting its feathers before flattening them out again.

No matter how carefully a Downy tends to its feathers, a year's wear-and-tear makes them worn and ragged. But that's no problem. Each summer, the Downy *molts,* it sheds its old feathers and grows a new set. The old ones fall out little by little, so that the Downy is never bald. It always has enough feathers to go about its work as the new feathers grow in.

24

Going South?

When winter sets in, most Downy Woodpeckers stay on their own ranges. Their *roosting holes,* or little caves carved into trees, protect them from the wind, snow, and rain. Using its bill, a woodpecker can tap for insects from inside its snug cave.

But Downy Woodpeckers that live in places that get very cold or snowy in the winter can't always find enough to eat. They *migrate,* or travel, to warmer places where they're sure to find food. Some just move down a mountain-side to a protected valley, while others fly farther south.

One bird-watcher found that some Downy Woodpeckers who usually flew south stayed on their ranges all winter when she put out *suet* for them. Suet, a hard animal fat, was the extra food the woodpeckers needed for the winter.

A steady supply of suet keeps Downy Woodpeckers healthy and happy during cold northern winters.

Two Kinds of Baths

Downy Woodpeckers don't like water very much, but they do take an occasional bath in the snow. On a warm, sunny day in late winter, you might find one dipping its bill into the wet snow, scooping the snow over its shoulder, and flapping its wings to spread it around.

There's another kind of bath that Downy Woodpeckers really like—a sunbath. A Downy will sprawl along a branch, facedown, with its wings spread half-open. It then lifts the feathers on its shoulders and neck, sticks its feet straight back out from under itself, and soaks up the sun's rays.

Whether a Downy is stretched out for a full-fledged sunbath or just sitting in a sunny spot, the warm rays of the sun are a welcome treat during the long winter.

Woodpecker Talk

The Downy doesn't sing in the way that many birds do. But it does make sounds and movements that tell other birds how it feels and what it's going to do. Some of a Downy's calls are loud and some are soft, while others are angry, frightened, or happy. Its loud "thick" call says, "Here I am," and can be heard a long way off. A sharp "tick-tick-tick" means that the bird is frightened. A loud "tickirrr" says "Danger!" and a soft "tut-tit-wi-tut-it" means "Hello".

Sounds are not the Downy's only way of communicating. It also raises and lowers its feathers and flies or moves in different ways to send messages. If it wants to chase another bird away, a Downy stretches out its head and neck, points its bill into the air, and whips its head from side to side. To other birds, the message is clear. "Stay away! This is my tree!"

Opposite page: *Sometimes a Downy will eat the seeds of plants, but perhaps the woodpecker on this flower stalk spies an even tastier treat—an ant or a beetle.*

Forest Drums

The Downy doesn't tap on wood only to find food. Another way that this bird uses its bill is to rap out messages on trees and hollow posts. Using its bill like a drumstick, a Downy raps in steady bursts. It can tap out 10 hits in a row, and then do it again and again, perhaps 15 times in a minute. In this way, the Downy can send many messages. It can announce where it is, or warn other animals to stay away, or even send out a call for a mate.

The rapid tapping of a Downy can be heard for quite a distance.

Time for a Mate

For Downy Woodpeckers, late winter and early spring is *mating season,* the time of year during which animals come together to produce young. The female begins to look for a mate by drumming out a message. If a male hears her, he drums back.

Before they settle down as a pair, the two Downy Woodpeckers chase each other from tree to tree and do a lot of drumming back and forth. They also fluff out their feathers, sometimes spreading their wings and tails, and they often wave their bodies from side to side.

Downy Woodpeckers mate for life. They nest on the same range, usually the male's, year after year. But because they live alone the rest of the time, even Downy Woodpeckers who have mated before go through the *courtship* process all over again at the beginning of each nesting season. Courtship is the behavior that animals engage in before they mate.

Hard-working Nest Builders

Downy Woodpeckers dig out a new *nest hole* each year. A nest hole is a hole dug in a tree to be used for a nest. The Downy pair each taps at many different trees before choosing a new site—but the female has the final say.

Downy Woodpeckers dig their holes high above the ground in dead wood. Often the female will choose a dead tree branch, a tall fence post, or a telephone pole. The male does most of the chiseling and the female helps. The Downy will dig for about 15 minutes at a time and then take a break to rest or eat before going back to work again.

Downy Woodpeckers work hard, but they also work carefully. First they dig a small cone-shaped hole in the middle of the spot that will be the nest entrance. When the hole gets a little deeper, a digging Downy must keep wiggling out backward, its feathers all ruffled, to toss billsful of wood chips over its shoulder.

Snug and Safe

When the Downy Woodpeckers are finished, they have a nest that will shelter them and their young from bad weather and keep them safe from most enemies. The entrance hole, usually a perfect circle, is about 1.5 inches (38 millimeters) in diameter. It's just big enough to let a grown-up Downy pass through. A passage leads straight in, then drops down to a wide nest hole. Some wood chips are left inside to make the floor soft enough for a nest.

Downy Woodpeckers take about two weeks to dig out their nest hole. But if other birds should succeed in driving them away close to egg-laying time, they can dig a new nest in two days of *very* hard work.

In between digging, the Downy Woodpeckers drum out the message that the small territory around their nest tree belongs to them and nobody else. And they drive away any bird that comes too close.

Cutaway of a Downy's nesting hole

A Family on the Way

The Downy female usually lays four or five small eggs. They are pure white, unlike many other bird eggs that are colored or mottled to blend in with their surroundings. Because the Downy's eggs are out of sight inside the nest hole, special coloring is not needed to keep them from being seen by *predators,* animals that hunt other animals for food.

The Downy female takes four to six days to lay her eggs. Once she's finished, a peaceful time begins. Both parents take long turns keeping the eggs warm and covered. During the entire time, the eggs are never left uncovered for more than a few minutes. Then at 12 days, the eggs begin to *hatch,* or crack open to produce babies.

Some torn bark provides this Downy easy access to an insect dinner.

Busy with Babies

Opposite page:
*Only occasionally
is there time for
a father Downy
to rest. Both
parents feed the
young, often
making dozens of
trips an hour to
find and deliver
food to their
babies.*

When they hatch, Downy *nestlings,* or young birds, are blind, featherless, and hungry. Their parents take turns feeding them. They bring food to the nest every two or three minutes all day long. While one parent searches for food, the other stays with the babies, protecting them and comforting them with soft calls.

At first the parent brings only one or two small ants. The parent climbs down into the nesting hole to feed one helpless baby at a time. But within a week, the nestlings are strong enough to climb the nest walls and meet their parents halfway. And by this time the menu has moved up to big insects. Soon, the babies are chipping loudly at the nest entrance as they wait for the next food delivery.

Until the young are grown, the father spends his nights in the nest while the mother sleeps nearby in another roosting hole. The father keeps the nest clean. The babies' droppings come out of their bodies in clean little sacks. The father picks up the sacks in his bill and carries them outside.

40

Finding Their Wings

After three weeks of hard work, the Downy Woodpecker parents know that it's almost time for their family to leave the nest. The young woodpeckers are almost as big as their parents and have grown a full set of feathers.

The adults encourage the young ones to leave. They begin to spend much of their time outside the nest. And they bring food only about 3 times an hour instead of 15 times. At last, hunger overcomes the young woodpeckers' fear of flying. They may hesitate when they launch their first flight, but soon they are as graceful in the air as their parents.

Once young Downy Woodpeckers are able to fly and move about outside their nest, they can watch their parents to learn other survival skills.

On Their Own

After young Downy Woodpeckers leave their nest, they never return to it. Each sleeps alone, hidden among the leaves of a nearby tree.

But they're far from ready for life on their own. Though they learn to fly and climb up trees very quickly, learning to feed themselves takes another three weeks. During that time, their parents help feed them. They find their young by following their calls. Those youngsters that are the closest or call the loudest get fed first.

As the young Downy Woodpeckers get better and better at looking after themselves, the family begins to move apart. By the middle of the summer, the young birds have grown up. They fly off to find ranges of their own and to prepare for the coming winter by digging roosting holes.

As for their parents, they return to their own separate ranges. There they take up their solitary fall and winter ways until spring draws them together again.

Opposite page: As with most birds, the flight of a Downy Woodpecker is made easier because of its hollow bones, which keep the bird's body light.

A Downy Long Life

The Downy, like most woodpeckers, is a tough bird. It's most in danger when it's young—as an egg, a nestling, or a very young bird without a roosting hole. Then animals—such as red squirrels—that are small enough to sneak into a Downy Woodpecker hole may try to make a Downy baby into a tender meal. Hunting birds such as hawks also are a threat to young woodpeckers.

But the Downy really has few serious enemies. If it survives its early days, it's quite likely to live to Downy old age—about eight or nine years. That's not surprising. After all, the Downy conveniently carries all the tools it needs to take care of itself in its life in the trees.

Words To Know

Courtship   Behavior animals engage in before mating.

Deciduous trees   Trees that lose their leaves in the fall.

Hatch   To crack open an egg to produce a baby.

Larva   The worm-like second stage of an insect's life, after it has hatched out of its egg. Also called a grub.

Markings   Patterns and colors in fur and feathers.

Mate   To come together to produce young. Also either member of an animal pair.

Mating Season   The time of year during which animals come together to produce young.

Migrate   To travel from one region to another.

Molt   To shed feathers or fur from time to time.

Nest hole   A hole dug in a tree by a bird or other animal for a nest.

Nestling   A young bird that has not yet left the nest.

Nostrils   Openings in a nose or bill that allow air into the body.

Parasite   A plant or animal that lives on another plant or animal.

Predator   An animal that hunts other animals for food.

Preening   Cleaning or grooming of feathers with the bill.

Range   Area that an animal or group of animals lives in and often defends from other animals of the same kind.

Roosting hole   A hole in a tree where a Downy Woodpecker sleeps at night and finds shelter in cold or wet weather.

Species   Class or kind of animals that have certain traits in common.

Suet   Hard animal fat.

Index